Saving Crumble

Story by Carmel Reilly
Illustrations by Cheryl Orsini

Contents

Chapter 1

On the Train

Dad and Frank got on the train.
They were going to see the children's art show at the Town Hall.
One of Frank's paintings was in the show.

Another family got on the train and stood next to Dad and Frank.
There was a girl, who was about Frank's age, and a little boy, who was about three.

The little boy carried a toy monkey.
He held it out to Frank.
“This is Crumble,” he said.

“Crumble is my brother’s best friend,”
the girl said to Frank.
“He goes with us everywhere!”

“Crumble is cute,” said Frank.
“I had a toy like that when I was little,
and I took him everywhere, too.”

Chapter 2

Dropping Crumble

After a few stops, the girl, the little boy and their mum got ready to get out.

Frank watched as the family got off the train. Then, just as the train doors started to shut, he saw Crumble on the floor.

"Look, Dad!" said Frank.
"The little boy dropped his toy monkey."

By the time Dad picked up the monkey, the train had started to move off. Frank could see the little boy outside. He looked very upset.

“I wish we could get the boy’s monkey back to him,” said Frank.

“The best thing to do,” said Dad,
“is to take the toy
to the Lost and Found Office.”

When Frank and Dad got off the train, they went to the Lost and Found Office.

"Oh, no, Dad," said Frank.
"The office is closed.
What do we do now?"

Dad looked at his watch.
"Let's go and see your painting," he said.
"The office should be open again
when we come back."

LOST AND FOUND
Closed for LUNCH

Chapter 3

A Surprise at the Art Show

Frank and Dad went along to the Town Hall.
The art show was in the main room
at the front of the building.

As they went inside,
Frank heard a child crying
somewhere across the room.
He looked around.

"Look, Dad!" he said.
"It's the little boy who lost the monkey."

Frank and Dad went over to the family.

"We found Crumble on the train," said Frank, giving the monkey to the little boy.

"You saved him!" said the boy.

"Thank you!" said his mum.
"But how did you know we were here?"

"We didn't know," said Dad.
"We came to see the show.
Frank has a painting here."

"So do I," said the girl. "It's this one."

"You won a prize!" said Frank.

"Look, Frank," said Dad.
"Your painting won a prize, too."

"What a great day!" said Frank.
"But the best bit was saving Crumble."